PUT YOUR CAT

ON THE
ALTAR

LASHAWNDA LOVE

Front cover image by Intellectual Designs by Lashawnda Love.
Book design by Intellectual Designs by Lashawnda Love.

First printing edition 2023.

Stork Publishing LLC.
700 South Boulevard Dr.
Bainbridge, Ga. 39819

www.lashawndashiree.info

PUBLISHING

Table of Contents

Introduction

I'm a 44-year-old Black woman, and I'm writing this book to extend a helping hand to those who might be struggling with celibacy during their single journey. Believe me, I understand the challenges, so let's have an open conversation and come up with a plan to keep you on the path of salvation, sanctity, and holiness. One quirky but profoundly important idea in this journey is "putting that CAT on the altar." But don't worry; we'll discuss what that means.

You know, this journey of celibacy and spiritual completeness can sometimes be a lot like dealing with a cat. Cats are curious creatures, always on the move, and they want what they want when they want it. Try to pet them when they're not in the mood, and you might get a swat for your troubles.

Well, isn't that how I acted with my singleness? I wanted companionship when it suited me. When the desires flared up, I was all in, but when I didn't, I was off chasing other things, just as curious as a cat. I'd keep myself occupied with work, hobbies, and everything else until I longed for the warmth of another's presence to cool the fires of my flesh.

You see, like cats, we humans also have our moments of desire and moments of independence. It's all part of the journey. Now, as we walk the path of celibacy and spiritual completeness, it's essential to delve into the biblical perspective on sex. Society portrays sex in countless ways, but as believers, we must align our understanding with God's teachings.

According to the Bible, sex is a divine gift, thoughtfully created by God as a beautiful and intimate expression of love, a treasure to be enjoyed within the sacred confines of marriage. In Genesis 2:24, we find the words, "Therefore a man shall leave his father and his mother and hold fast to his wife, and they shall become one flesh." This verse beautifully underscores the unity and intimacy that sexual relations are meant to nurture within the secure bounds of a marital relationship.

Let's imagine we're having a conversation, just you and me, pondering these questions together:

1. Why Did God Create Sex? Have you ever wondered why God gave us the gift of sex? Is it only for making babies, or is there more to it? It's a question that leads us to a profound understanding of God's design. While procreation is indeed one aspect of it, there's more beneath the surface. Sex isn't just about reproducing; it's a beautiful and intimate connection between husband and wife. It's a way for two people deeply in love to express their feelings physically and emotionally. It's a reminder of the union they share. In Genesis 2:24, we read, "Therefore a man shall leave his father and his mother and hold fast to his wife, and they shall become one flesh." This verse highlights the unity and intimacy that sexual relations are meant to foster within the bounds of a marital relationship.

2. What Does the Bible Say About Staying Pure? We'll explore passages like 1 Thessalonians 4:3-5, which highlight the importance of avoiding sexual immorality. Let's see what wisdom we can gain from these teachings. These passages serve as guideposts for

maintaining sexual purity. They remind us that God desires us to keep our bodies holy and away from sexual immorality. It's not about being restrictive; it's about protecting the sanctity of sex and reserving it for the sacred covenant of marriage.

3. How Does Sex Connect to Love and Commitment? It's interesting to think about the link between love and sex within the boundaries of marriage. Have you thought about how this intimate act can deepen the connection between spouses, both emotionally and spiritually? When we view sex as a gift shared exclusively between a husband and wife, it takes on a whole new dimension. It becomes a powerful expression of love and commitment, deepening the bond between partners, emotionally, spiritually, and even physically. It's a way of saying, "I am entirely yours," fostering a level of intimacy that's hard to replicate outside the marriage covenant.

4. What Happens When You Stray? We'll also consider the serious topic of what can occur when sex happens outside of marriage. How might it affect your spiritual and emotional well-being? It's important to ponder

these aspects as we continue our journey. Straying from the path of sexual purity can have profound consequences. It can lead to feelings of guilt, remorse, and emotional turmoil. It can damage your relationship with God and even with your partner. By exploring these consequences, we can better understand why preserving sexual purity is not about restriction but about protection and nurturing the precious gift that is sex within marriage.

Sex Within Marriage: Ah, now let's delve into the beautiful realm of sex within marriage – a topic celebrated in the Bible with heartfelt enthusiasm. Picture this: Proverbs 5:18-19 tenderly whispering to us, "Let your fountain be blessed, and rejoice in the wife of your youth, a lovely deer, a graceful doe. Let her breasts fill you at all times with delight; be intoxicated always in her love." Isn't that captivating imagery? It's an invitation to celebrate the divine connection between two lovers, deeply rooted in the commitment of marriage. Beyond the physical realm, this act becomes spiritual and profound. It's not merely an expression of love but a declaration of unwavering devotion. Imagine it as a vibrant tapestry that mirrors the extraordinary relationship between Christ and His church (Ephesians 5:31-32). It's like a love song, a dance of the soul, and a sacred promise all rolled into one.

Now, as we conclude this part of our conversation, it's essential to remember that sex, in itself, isn't a negative thing. It's a precious gift from God. Although I'm married now, I remember the journey to get here. I stumbled as a single individual, but it's never too late for a turnaround. For those of you still on that path, I encourage you to place all your CATs on the altar. Let's do it together, and let's flourish in the light of His guidance.

"Now, let's bow our heads in prayer, my dear sisters. *Heavenly Father, as we explore the topic of sex and its role in our lives, we humbly seek Your guidance and understanding. We recognize that sex is a precious gift from You, intended to bring joy and intimacy within the loving embrace of marriage.*

Lord, grant us the wisdom and strength to honor Your divine design for sex and to refrain from any form of sexual immorality. Instill in us the courage to maintain purity in our thoughts, words, and actions, and to stand firm in waiting for the right time and the right person, as You have divinely ordained.

We also lift up those among us who may have encountered struggles in this area. May they find solace and healing in Your boundless grace. May our understanding of sex be deeply rooted in Your Word, reflecting love, commitment, and unity within the sacred bond of matrimony.

In the name of our Lord and Savior, Jesus, we earnestly pray. Amen."

As we embark on this journey together, let's continue exploring the profound biblical principles that illuminate our path toward celibacy and spiritual wholeness. Understanding God's viewpoint on sex is a vital step in aligning our lives with His divine purpose.

Chapter 1

Let's Talk About Sex

Sex, sex - there, I've said it. Now, let's talk about it. These words might make you squirm in your seat, but that's perfectly normal. I'm not here to judge or make you uncomfortable. Instead, I'm here as a fellow traveler on life's journey, a 44-year-old Black woman, sharing my experiences and insights in the hope that they can resonate with you.

Picture this: after 23 years of marriage, I found myself suddenly single. It was a shocking and bewildering change. I was thrust into a world of dating and intimacy outside the familiar boundaries of marriage. What made it even more challenging was the fact that I was dealing with a body that had been exposed to intimacy before. Managing these desires became one of the most formidable challenges of my life.

In sincere prayer, I earnestly sought God's guidance and strength to navigate a life of holiness while single. It reminds me of a time, a few years back when I found myself repeatedly counseling an individual year after year. They were facing relationship issues, and after a while, I couldn't help but blurt out the truth: "Your cat is on fire, sis, and it needs to be placed firmly on the altar until it cools down. In fact, I even suggested she pin it down and hog-tie it to that altar!" I couldn't help but chuckle at my own frustration. I knew it sounded funny, but sometimes you reach a point where you just can't hold back anymore.

Do you see how it's often second nature to provide guidance to others, but what do you do when the counsel you're offering reflects right back at you? Who would have thought that I would have to "EAT THE CAKE, ANNIE MAE"? I recall those moments of self-reflection, realizing that my own actions mirrored what I was advising against. I'd hear that inner voice saying, "You know you're wrong for that," and I'd promise to repent, but I'd find myself stuck in the same cycle. It was a humbling experience, one that made me recognize that I had taken God's grace for granted. I had assumed I had it all figured out or that I was exempt from putting my CAT on the altar. This journey of self-discovery had its share of bumps and bruises, but it was a transformative path toward becoming the woman God intended me to be.

And so, the seed for this Book was planted. It's a platform for me to share my experiences, my tribulations, and my victories with you. It's about sparking a conversation, a dialogue that addresses the challenges of controlling our bodies, particularly when they've been exposed to intimacy.

I know I'm not the only one who has had this issue and struggle. What I was faced with was knowing God's word and then applying God's word. How and why was I unable to put my own CAT on the Altar? Truthfully, there really isn't any excuse. Being that we are all free-will agents, God allows us to make these horrible decisions and then we have to deal with the effects of our decision.

Sex is a good thing but must be used in the proper context. God wants us to experience these pleasures but with our spouse. What I needed at the time was to set boundaries, have a practical plan to date, and heal from issues that were deeper than sex. There are times when we use sex to cover up a much deeper issue. My deeper issues stemmed from a spirit of rejection, low self-esteem, poor self-worth, depression, and unprocessed trauma. Now you see why it was so easy for me to cover up my hurt with sex.

I remember when I was in the middle of an affair and how powerful I felt because I was giving my body up willingly at command. This made me feel powerful, as if I was in control of the individual. We all know that trying to control others is a form of witchcraft (Galatians 3:1). I even thought that when I did marry the person that it would be the sex that kept us together, but little did I know sex is not the fixer to all our problems. Even in this situation, sex was used as a weapon in the wrong way.

Do you see all the layers? We have so many layers, and we use sex as well as other things to deal with our issues instead of seeking true healing. Healing and knowing your worth is a must, and I pray that you will be able to heal as you turn these pages. Healing will help you place and keep your cat on the Altar.

Now, let's dive deeper into the significance of this concept. The idea of putting your "cat" on the altar may sound puzzling, but it's rooted in biblical principles. Just as in ancient times, people would offer sacrifices to God as an act of worship and surrender, we too are called to offer ourselves—our bodies, desires, and hearts—as living sacrifices (Romans 12:1). This act of consecration aligns with God's plan for our lives.

When you put your "cat" on the altar, you're not only acknowledging your reliance on God but also expressing your willingness to submit your physical and emotional needs to His guidance. It's an act of faith, a way of saying, "Lord, I trust You to guide me in matters of intimacy and relationships." This step, however unconventional it may seem, can be transformative.

My journey of self-discovery and transformation didn't happen overnight, and it wasn't without challenges. But with faith, perseverance, and a willingness to put my "cat" on the altar, I found strength and healing.

If we turn to 1 Corinthians 6:19-20, we find these words: "Or do you not know that your body is a temple of the Holy Spirit within you, whom you have from God? You are not your own, for you were bought with a price. So glorify God in your body." These verses underscore the idea that our bodies are not our own but are temples of the Holy Spirit. By putting our "cats" on the altar, we're glorifying God in our bodies and recognizing His ownership over us.

The journey ahead may not be easy, but it's a path filled with purpose and transformation. As we continue, I'll offer you more insights, personal experiences, and guidance to help you navigate the challenges of living a life of singleness and holiness. Together, we'll explore the power of faith, the importance of community, and the healing of past wounds, all while keeping our "cats" where they belong—on the altar.

Chapter 2

Why It's So Important

Ladies, there's a remarkable journey ahead for you, and you'll face all kinds of challenges on the path. The enemy will throw everything at you to keep you from becoming the amazing person God has in mind for you, your absolute best self. It's important to recognize that many of us have gone through experiences involving intimacy, whether inside or outside of marriage. This makes the task of maintaining celibacy until your husband finds you an extraordinary challenge.

The key understanding here is that God wants you to remain celibate until your future husband finds you. Yes, you heard it right; that cat needs to stay put until your husband finds you. God's wisdom in this choice is beautifully articulated in scriptures like Proverbs 18:22, which says, "He who finds a wife finds a good thing and obtains favor from the Lord." This is about waiting for the man who will recognize your worth, the one whom God intends to bless you with.

Now, it goes even deeper than you might think, and the concept of soul ties is not to be taken lightly. God is trying to keep us from being entangled in soul ties with multiple people and their connections because He comprehends the significance of soul ties. The emotional and spiritual bonds that form when you engage intimately with someone are profound, creating connections that extend far beyond the physical. So, when God urges you to wait for your future husband, He's looking out for you in ways you may not fully realize yet.

Soul Ties: The Deeper Connection

Soul ties, often discussed in the context of relationships and intimacy, are a concept that dives into the complex dynamics of human connections. These ties go way beyond just the physical aspects; they include emotional, spiritual, and psychological elements that bind two individuals together, leaving a profound impact long after the physical relationship has ended.

When you engage in intimacy with someone other than your spouse, it's essential to understand that it's not merely a physical act. It's a profound merging of two souls, almost like becoming as interconnected as "bone of each other's bone and flesh of each other's flesh," as described in Genesis 2:24. This spiritual and emotional union forms a connection that goes beyond the physical dimension, leading to what we commonly refer to as a soul tie.

Let's delve deeper into this concept. Soul ties are like invisible bonds between people, forged through shared experiences, emotional connections, and intimate moments. They aren't just a fleeting feeling; they can become a deep, lasting connection that impacts your life in profound ways. This connection can remain long after the physical relationship ends, influencing your thoughts, emotions, and actions.

In fact, studies have shown that soul ties can have a significant impact on an individual's emotional well-being.

People who have experienced soul ties often report feelings of longing, emotional turmoil, and a sense of being unable to move forward. These bonds can lead to a constant sense of attachment to someone, even when it's no longer a healthy or viable connection.

Understanding soul ties can shed light on why it's crucial to wait for the right person, your future spouse, before engaging in intimate relationships. These ties are not easily severed, and becoming entangled in multiple soul ties can lead to emotional baggage that affects your future relationships. It's about protecting your heart, mind, and spirit from unnecessary entanglements that can hinder your path to a fulfilling and God-centered relationship. So, by waiting for your future husband, you're not only honoring God's plan but also safeguarding your own emotional and spiritual well-being.

The Complexity of Soul Ties

Soul ties are not limited to the immediate couple; they cast a wide-reaching net that involves all the individuals with whom your partner has shared intimate connections. To understand this better, picture a complex tapestry interwoven with the experiences, emotions, and histories of numerous people. If your partner has had these connections with, say, a hundred different individuals, you essentially become interconnected not just with your partner but with all those hundred others.

This intricate interconnectedness can lead to a wide range of emotions and complexities that often arise when dealing with soul ties. It's like inheriting a piece of the emotional baggage, desires, and wounds of every person in your partner's history. This isn't a choice you make consciously; it's an inherent consequence of engaging in intimate relationships.

To illustrate, imagine a scenario where a person enters a relationship with a partner who has had a series of previous partners, all with their unique experiences, traumas, and emotional connections. Each of these past relationships has left an imprint on your partner's soul, affecting their emotional and spiritual makeup.

As you become involved with this partner, you aren't just entering a relationship with them; you're stepping into the complex emotional web that includes the experiences and emotional bonds they share with their past partners. In a sense, you become interconnected with all these people, even though you've never met them. This intricate connection can bring forth a multitude of emotions, desires, and wounds, leading to a complicated emotional landscape that you now must navigate.

The Effects of Soul Ties

The consequences of these intertwined connections can be far-reaching, impacting your emotional, mental, and physical well-being. Here are some potential effects of soul ties:

1. **Mood Swings:** Soul ties can lead to unexplained mood swings and emotional instability as you inadvertently absorb the emotional energies of past connections. This can affect your emotional resilience and overall well-being.

2. **Unresolved Traumas:** The emotional baggage from past relationships can surface in your current relationship, leading to misunderstandings and conflicts that may not seem directly related. Unresolved traumas from past soul ties can hinder your personal growth and your ability to build a healthy relationship.

3. **Diseases and Health Issues:** Studies have shown that sexually transmitted diseases (STDs) can be transmitted through soul ties when one partner has had intimate

relationships with infected individuals. Statistics reveal
that a significant percentage of new STD cases result
from such connections.

Statistics on Soul Ties and Health Issues:

- According to the Centers for Disease Control and
  Prevention (CDC), approximately 20 million new STD
  cases are reported each year in the United States alone.

- A study published in the Journal of Sexual Medicine
  found that individuals who had multiple sexual partners
  were at a higher risk of contracting STDs.

- A study conducted by the World Health Organization
  (WHO) reported that the transmission of STDs can
  occur not only through sexual contact but also via
  emotional and spiritual connections between
  individuals.

Understanding the depth and complexity of soul ties
underscores the importance of waiting for your future spouse.
By doing so, you're choosing to protect your heart, mind, and
spirit from becoming entangled in a web of interconnected
emotions and experiences. This decision allows you to embark
on a new relationship with a clean slate, unburdened by the

emotional baggage of past connections. It's a step toward ensuring your emotional and physical well-being as you seek a fulfilling and healthy relationship.

The Challenge of Detachment

Now, when it comes to finally breaking free from these soul ties, think of it as trying to unravel that complex web I mentioned earlier. It's not as simple as just moving on because you're not only connected to your partner; you're intertwined with all the people they've been with before. This intertwinement often lies at the heart of the issue, causing inner turmoil, emotional conflict, and a feeling of being trapped.

You see, the challenge of breaking these soul ties is made even more difficult because they're not confined to just the physical realm. They go deeper, involving your emotions, memories, and even spiritual bonds that persist long after the physical relationship has ended. As a result, many folks find themselves struggling to move forward, held back by these invisible threads that keep them connected to their past. It's like being caught in a spider's web, trying to free yourself from the sticky, clinging strands. This inner struggle and emotional baggage can often affect your present relationships and your overall well-being. So, ladies, it's crucial to understand the complexities of soul ties and the challenges they bring into our lives. This is why God is guiding you to wait for your future husband, helping you avoid these intricate entanglements and emotional complexities as you journey toward a fulfilling and healthy relationship. So, ladies, remember, that's why that cat needs to stay on the altar.

Women typically experience a deeper emotional connection in relationships, which can make separation more challenging for them. When a soul tie is formed, women may invest a significant part of their emotional and spiritual selves in the relationship. The emotional attachment can lead to a sense of responsibility and connection that is hard to sever. The complexity of a soul tie, intertwined with shared emotions, memories, and spiritual bonds, makes it difficult for women to move forward after a breakup.

Men, on the other hand, may initially appear to move on more easily. This is not because they are immune to the effects of soul ties but because societal expectations often encourage emotional restraint in men. Men might not openly express their struggles or emotions after a breakup, but it doesn't mean they aren't affected. The emotional weight of these connections can silently weigh on them, impacting their ability to form new, healthy relationships.

In summary, women and men experience soul ties differently due to societal expectations, emotional connection, and the way they handle separation. It's important to recognize that both genders can be deeply affected by soul ties, and understanding these differences can help individuals navigate the challenges of moving on and maintaining celibacy.

Building upon the discussion of celibacy and soul ties, we can find further clarity and guidance in these scriptures:

1. **Ephesians 5:31:** "Therefore a man shall leave his father and mother and hold fast to his wife, and the two shall become one flesh." This verse reinforces the concept of becoming one flesh in the context of marriage.

2. **Matthew 19:5-6:** "Therefore a man shall leave his father and his mother and hold fast to his wife, and the two shall become one flesh'? So they are no longer two but one flesh. What therefore God has joined together, let not man separate." These verses emphasize the sacred union of marriage and the oneness it brings.

3. **1 Thessalonians 4:3-5:** "For this is the will of God,

your sanctification: that you abstain from sexual immorality; that each one of you know how to control his own body in holiness and honor, not in the passion of lust like the Gentiles who do not know God." This passage stresses the importance of sexual purity and self-control.

4. **Hebrews 13:4:** "Let marriage be held in honor among all, and let the marriage bed be undefiled, for God will judge the sexually immoral and adulterous." It underscores the sanctity of marriage and the consequences of sexual immorality.

These passages collectively stress the importance of staying celibate, preserving purity, and understanding the repercussions of engaging in sexual immorality. They lay the foundation for our future discussions on Putting that cat on the altar celibacy and soul ties in the upcoming chapters.

As we continue through the chapters ahead, we'll delve deeper into the intricate challenges associated with celibacy, explore strategies to safeguard your spiritual and emotional well-being, and discuss practical methods for navigating the path of faith and relationships. This journey is one we'll embark on together, guided by understanding, compassion,

and faith as our beacons of light. It's not easy, but put it on the
altar.

Chapter 3

Single but Don't Know How to Mingle

Listen, I'm not here to cast stones or pass judgment because, as they say, "He who is without sin, cast the first stone." However, I can share my own experiences with you. During the brief period when I found myself single, it felt like there was a proverbial radar on me. Suddenly, all sorts of peculiar individuals, mostly men, seemed to come out of the woodwork, eager to enter into a relationship with me, as if I were fresh meat.

I couldn't help but wonder: Did I give off an air of desperation? Did my posts on social media scream "desperado"? What was it that attracted all these people to me? To my surprise, a staggering 98% of them were not men of God; they were not godly individuals. Like many of you, I fell into the trap of dating without establishing boundaries. Being married for so long had conditioned me to rush into the "marry zone" with anyone I came into contact with, skipping the friend zone entirely.

Before I knew it, I found myself intimately involved, cooking, and doing all the things that should have been reserved for my husband. It contradicted everything I had been taught, and deep down, I knew it was wrong. However, in the moment, I lacked the willpower to abstain from being intimate with someone who wasn't my husband. It forced me to confront an uncomfortable question: What was driving me to seek intimacy prematurely, and what was preventing me from waiting?

Even when I tried Christian dating, I found myself facing an uphill battle. I was lonely, scrolling through TikTok one day, and I stumbled upon Lecrae talking about a Christian dating app. I thought, "Why not give it a try?" I even went so far as to pay for a subscription. I just wanted someone to talk to; the loneliness was eating away at me.

To my disappointment, even the men I encountered on this Christian dating app seemed far from being true Christians. In fact, they were so far from it that I found myself in some of the most peculiar and unexpected relationship situations. I was completely unprepared for the challenges of dating as a Christian woman.

As if that weren't enough, I had all sorts of predators sliding into my Facebook inbox. It felt like all the wrong individuals were coming my way. Dating as a Christian woman turned out to be an incredibly challenging journey. Even though we know we shouldn't engage in sexual activity, many of us still do. We indulge in it and then seek forgiveness later.

So, what's the problem here? It boils down to several factors: a lack of boundaries, a lack of self-control, a misunderstanding of our worth, and a forgetfulness that we are the prize worth waiting for. In today's culture, waiting isn't something that many of us are eager to do. However, it's often the best course of action.

Waiting isn't about being idle; it's about waiting with purpose and in purpose. Here are some things you can do while waiting:

Work on Yourself: Invest in personal growth and self-improvement. Devote time to discovering your strengths and weaknesses, and strive to become the best version of yourself.

Get a Life Coach or Mentor: Seek guidance and support from someone who can help you navigate life's challenges. A mentor or life coach can provide valuable insights and hold you accountable on your journey.

Go Back to School: Consider furthering your education or acquiring new skills. Education opens doors and can lead to fulfilling career opportunities.

Learn a New Craft or Hobby: Explore your interests and passions. Cultivating a hobby or mastering a new skill can be a fulfilling and productive way to spend your time.

Date Yourself: Treat yourself to the things you enjoy; self-love is essential. Take time for self-care, pampering, and pursuing activities that bring you joy and fulfillment.

Pray: Strengthen your relationship with God through prayer. Seek guidance, solace, and spiritual growth in your connection with the Divine.

Go on Trips: Explore new places and create memorable experiences. Traveling can broaden your horizons, provide fresh perspectives, and offer opportunities for self-discovery.

Read God's Word: Deepen your understanding of scripture. Spend time in prayerful study of the Bible to nourish your spiritual life.

Fast and Pray: Use fasting as a means of spiritual growth and self-discipline. Fasting can help you develop self-control and draw closer to God.

Develop Yourself: Become a virtuous woman so that when your husband finds you, he will discover a woman who has grown, transformed, and is truly worth waiting for. Focus on building your character and living a life aligned with your values.

Now, let's address an important perspective: We are supposed to be in hiding until our husbands find us. Proverbs tells us, "He who finds..." Perhaps where I was going wrong is that I was looking for someone to fill my void. I wanted a quick fix for my loneliness and the ache I felt late at night. I sought to fix the problem, and the problem was me. Can you relate?

In many ways, our desire for instant gratification can lead us astray. We look for immediate solutions to our pain, loneliness, and desires, often overlooking the importance of waiting for the right person, God's chosen one for us. Waiting isn't always easy, but it's in the waiting that we discover our true worth and allow God to work in our lives.

This journey is not an easy one, but it's a path of self-discovery, healing, and growth. It's about becoming the best version of yourself and aligning your life with God's purpose for you. While waiting may not always be easy, it is undoubtedly the right thing to do. It's about choosing to wait with purpose, intent, and faith, knowing that God has a plan for your life, and He is preparing you for a love that is worth the wait.

Chapter 4

Let's Have an Honest Chat About You

It's time for a candid conversation about you. Let's talk about your challenges, dreams, and what makes you tick. You might have pondered some of these questions before, just as I have. So, let's get real and explore them together.

First things first, have you ever wondered why we sometimes feel incomplete without someone else in our lives? Why isn't being single and drawing closer to the Lord enough on its own? These are questions that have crossed my mind, and I suspect they've crossed yours too.

You see, for much of my life, I was the person everyone turned to for help, advice, and support. I was the one who listened, who cared deeply about other people's issues, dreams, and desires. But in the midst of all this outward focus, there was a part of me I hadn't paid much attention to. Turning that focus inward was a challenge, but it was a pivotal step in my journey.

So, what's the plan? First, acknowledge and repent to God if you're sorry for your actions. Let Him know that you need His intervention. You can't do this alone. Next, create a plan. For instance, when you're dating, ensure you're never alone with someone. Take someone with you or meet in public places. Avoid situations that make you vulnerable to temptation. Remember, you're not as strong as you may think, and it's better to take precautions.

I began by praying and asking God for help. I needed His guidance to put my cat (body) on the altar, to control my fleshly desires, and to become the woman of God He called me to be. This marked the beginning of a fresh focus on self.

I decided it was high time to explore and understand myself better. I grabbed a pen and wrote a heartfelt letter, asking myself questions like: "What genuinely brings you joy? What's your all-time favorite comfort food? Do you have a go-to color that resonates with your spirit? What dreams have you tucked away, waiting to be pursued?"

With this newfound commitment to self-discovery, I immersed myself in my own world. I shifted my priorities away from the pursuit of a romantic relationship and redirected my energy inward. Every day, I reminded God of my desire to get married, to not remain single forever, but also my commitment to self-improvement during this season of waiting.

I took proactive steps to prioritize personal growth. I sought therapy to address past issues that had been weighing on my heart. I invested time in activities I hadn't explored before, trying out things that genuinely made me happy. I started dating myself—indulging in activities that brought me joy. I even ventured into travel, exploring new destinations and creating cherished memories along the way.

But I also learned the importance of staying clear of people, places, and situations that could potentially lead me astray. I remembered the Bible's wisdom that tells us to resist the devil, and he will flee. What trips you up is precisely what you need to avoid. If I found myself in a conversation that was steering toward topics I knew weren't edifying, I changed the subject or ended the conversation. I learned to discern when something wasn't good for my spiritual journey and had the strength to walk away.

In interactions with potential partners, I made sure never to be alone with them. I recognized that my own strength wasn't sufficient to resist temptation. I understood the value of having an accountability partner, someone who could help me stay on the right path. I made a conscious effort to steer clear of situations that could compromise my commitment, because, as they say, "It's easier to avoid temptation than to resist it."

Now, here's a valuable piece of advice I can offer you: Just as Romans 12:1 encourages us, present your body, your very self, as a living sacrifice to God. It's like saying, "God, I acknowledge my struggle with my flesh. I need Your divine help to overcome them, to resist the things that lead me astray. My ultimate goal is to honor Your name, so please assist me," and rest assured, God is more than willing to help, but it all begins with acknowledging that there's a challenge, even if you're unsure of its extent.

When you're in conversations, be honest with the other person. Make sure you share similar moral and Christian backgrounds and values. This understanding will help when you explain your decision to abstain from premarital sex. If someone pressures you and that's all they talk about, consider finding someone else to converse with.

Prayer should be your daily practice, not just on this journey but throughout life. Pray fervently and seek God's strength to overcome temptation. Remember, there are Scriptures that guide us in this journey, and they offer valuable insights. Here are a few:

1. **1 Corinthians 6:18:** "Flee from sexual immorality. Every other sin a person commits is outside the body, but the sexually immoral person sins against his own body."

2. **1 Corinthians 10:13:** "No temptation has overtaken you that is not common to man. God is faithful, and he will not let you be tempted beyond your ability, but with the temptation, he will also provide the way of escape, that you may be able to endure it."

3. **Proverbs 4:23:** "Keep your heart with all vigilance, for from it flow the springs of life."

4. **1 Thessalonians 4:3-5:** "For this is the will of God, your sanctification: that you abstain from sexual

immorality; that each one of you know how to control his own body in holiness and honor, not in the passion of lust like the Gentiles who do not know God."

5. **Hebrews 13:4:** "Let marriage be held in honor among all, and let the marriage bed be undefiled, for God will judge the sexually immoral and adulterous."

As you keep moving forward on this journey, consider these practical steps and scripture references as your guiding lights. Always remember that you're not traveling this path alone. God's grace is abundant and empowers you to navigate the waiting process with strength and faith. Placing that cat on the altar is gradually becoming easier and more achievable. It's something that you simply must do, and with God's help, you can.

Chapter 5

The Power of Community

Let's talk about the importance of having a solid support system as you navigate the path of singleness and holiness. We've all heard the age-old saying, "It takes a village," and when it comes to your journey, this couldn't be more accurate.

Why Your Support System Matters

You might not realize just how crucial your family and friends are until you face challenging times. As a single woman, it's incredibly important to surround yourself with people who will uplift and support you on your journey. Why spend time with someone who encourages behavior that goes against your values when you can have a circle of supportive, like-minded believers by your side?

Reaching Out for Help

Putting your cat on the altar can be easier if you reach out for help. You can't be out here alone. I personally found this extremely helpful when I realized I was going about things the wrong way. I confided in someone about what was going on and gave them permission to check me if they saw, heard, or felt like I was veering off the path I had committed to. Having someone to hold you accountable and provide encouragement is a game-changer on this journey. It's like having a dependable co-pilot on a flight; they help keep you on course.

Remember, you don't have to do this alone. Seek out individuals who share your faith and values, and let them be your support system. Open up to a close friend, a mentor, or a fellow church member. Find those who will walk this path with you, offering guidance and standing with you in times of struggle.

Together, we can navigate the challenges of maintaining your commitment to celibacy and upholding your faith, and put your cat on the altar. Building a strong support system is a significant step in this journey, one that can make the path much smoother and less lonely.

The Role of Community in Your Journey

Living a life of holiness and contentment while single isn't a path you should walk alone. In fact, having a strong, supportive community can be the wind beneath your wings. These individuals can provide you with not only encouragement but also crucial guidance and unwavering accountability. For me, my parents, siblings, and friends were my anchors during my season of singleness. Who serves as your anchor? When you surround yourself with like-hearted individuals who share your faith and values, the impact on your journey can be truly remarkable.

Finding Your Accountability Partner

Have you ever considered the idea of having an accountability partner? Think of them as your trusty co-pilot on this journey. Your accountability partner can be a friend or mentor, someone willing to walk this path alongside you. They're there to help keep you on course, lift you up in prayer, and lend a compassionate ear when challenges arise. Together, you can nurture your faith and grow in holiness. It's like having a wingman for your spiritual journey. This person should be someone you can trust wholeheartedly, someone who genuinely loves you and has your best interests at heart.

Support Groups: Your Tribe Beyond Borders

Believe it or not, platforms like Facebook are perfect places to discover support groups. In today's interconnected world, finding support groups designed for Christian singles, whether locally or online, has never been more accessible. These groups offer a sense of belonging, akin to a virtual or physical tribe. Here, you can share your experiences, unveil your challenges, and celebrate your triumphs. These groups are overflowing with inspiration and packed with practical advice, much like a treasure chest brimming with wisdom.

Your Church Family: The Original Support Network

Your church, your spiritual haven, is also an invaluable source of community. Engaging in church activities, participating in small groups, or using your talents to contribute to ministries can foster a profound sense of belonging. Your pastor and fellow church members should always be sources of love, support, and answers. Personally, I find comfort in the fact that I can approach Apostle Delesa Patterson, my spiritual leader at Kingdom Ambassadors Ministries in Thomasville, GA, and ask her anything.

In closing, let me emphasize the incredible power of community on your journey. With the support and accountability of like-minded believers, the guidance of the Holy Spirit, a strong sense of conviction, and a healthy fear of the Lord, you can confidently take that essential step to put your cat on the altar. The path may have its challenges, but remember, you're not alone. Your community stands with you, offering encouragement, prayer, and unwavering support as you commit to living a life of holiness and faith. Together, we'll take those transformative steps toward a future filled with purpose, self-discovery, and a deep, unwavering connection with God.

Chapter 6

Healing Past Wounds - A Journey to Wholeness

Let's talk about something that's quite significant on your path to living a holy and fulfilling single life: the process of healing past wounds and emotional baggage. Many of us carry deep hurts and scars from our past, and it's essential to address them to move forward with joy and wholeness.

Recognizing Your Emotional Baggage

It's time for some self-reflection. Take a moment to think about the past experiences or relationships that have left emotional scars on your heart. Acknowledging these wounds is the crucial first step towards healing. I know it might sound tough, but this was the single most important thing that brought healing into my life and helped me place my CAT (my body) on the altar. It all began with confessing the hurt and guarding my heart. The way you guard your heart may look different for each person, as everyone's baggage is unique. In my case, the pain was so intense that I couldn't bear to communicate, see, hear from, or respond to the individual for a solid two years.

Let's dive into a crucial aspect of this journey – getting professional help when you need it. It's essential to know that seeking professional assistance doesn't mean you're "crazy." Instead, it's a brave step toward healing and self-improvement.

I didn't always realize how much help I needed to sort through the complexities of my life. It was only when I started watching Dr. RC Blakes on YouTube during my journey that I saw the depth of my own brokenness. He became my daily source of wisdom, a bit like my "YouTube therapist." Eventually, I took the step to reach out to Better Help and schedule a session with a professional therapist.

Just like me, you can benefit from the support of a trained therapist or counselor when dealing with deep emotional pain. Therapy is a valuable tool for healing and personal growth. In my case, I combined spiritual counseling, professional therapy, and self-deliverance processes. I realized the importance of seeking help and didn't make any excuses. This decision can genuinely make a positive impact on your path to wholeness and healing. Remember, you're not alone on this journey, and professional help can be an essential part of your healing process.

Forgiveness and Release

Forgiveness is an essential step in the healing process, and it holds incredible power. It's about breaking free from the emotional grip that others' actions have on your heart. This process doesn't mean you're condoning their wrongdoings, but rather, you're liberating yourself from the pain's hold.

In my own journey of healing, a pivotal moment arrived when I chose to write a heartfelt letter to the person who had caused me hurt. I poured all my emotions and thoughts into that letter, seeking forgiveness. Then, I engaged in a symbolic act by burning it. Watching the flames consume the letter brought an overwhelming sense of release and freedom.

Additionally, I embarked on a journey of self-forgiveness. I apologized to myself for holding onto the pain inflicted by that individual. This self-forgiveness became a crucial part of my progress toward moving forward.

As I navigated my healing process, I decided to share my experiences and insights on various online platforms, such as YouTube (Lashawnda Shiree Love) and TikTok (Dr. Lashawnda Love). This journey had its share of challenges, with both support and backlash. However, the healing I experienced through sharing my journey was profound.

The support I received came from all directions - encounters at the grocery store, gas station, emails, texts, and phone calls. It was a testament to the healing power of sharing and connecting with a community that understood my journey.

Understanding the weight of unforgiveness is equally crucial. Unforgiveness can lead to a myriad of physical and emotional issues, including increased stress, anxiety, and even physical ailments. The longer you hold onto unforgiveness, the more it can impact your well-being. It's a burden that can weigh you down.

In Matthew 6:14-15, the Bible tells us, "For if you forgive other people when they sin against you, your heavenly Father will also forgive you. But if you do not forgive others their sins, your Father will not forgive your sins." This scripture emphasizes the importance of forgiveness in our spiritual journey.

Statistically, studies have shown that practicing forgiveness can lead to better mental and physical health. It reduces stress, lowers blood pressure, and improves overall well-being. So, forgiving isn't just about setting others free; it's about freeing yourself from the chains of unforgiveness.

Embracing forgiveness is a transformative step in your journey towards healing and wholeness. It's about breaking the cycle of pain and allowing yourself to move forward with a lighter heart and a brighter spirit. So, as you continue on your path of healing, remember the tremendous power of forgiveness and how it can set you free.

Renewing Your Mind

Embrace a mindset of healing and renewal. Replace those negative thought patterns with positive affirmations and Scripture. God's Word offers constant comfort and healing to those who are hurting.

I'd like to suggest a helpful tool that you can incorporate into your own personal journey. In my own path of personal growth and healing, I found that utilizing a mobile app that sent uplifting affirmations to my phone every hour was particularly beneficial. When these affirmations appeared, I made a conscious effort to pause, recite them, truly embrace their messages, and then carry that positivity with me throughout the day. This straightforward practice gradually transformed my thought patterns, guiding them towards a more positive and healing direction. It's a simple yet effective technique that you might find helpful.

In addition to the affirmations, I made a daily commitment to immerse myself in the Word. I downloaded the Bible Experience, featuring various artists and famous figures reading the Scriptures, and I listened to it daily. I recited positive words and Scriptures as a part of my daily routine. Each morning as I woke up, I would remind myself, "You will be happy, whole, and heal completely. You are still a wife and a great mother. When your husband finds you, he will find you whole, with no baggage to carry into your new marriage." This practice reinforced my healing and personal growth journey.

As we reach the end of our journey to place our Cats on the altar, I want to leave you with some encouraging affirmations and comforting scriptures. These affirmations are potent statements that can assist you in shifting from negative thinking to a more positive mindset, allowing you to welcome God's love and grace.

Affirmations

1. I release all pain and embrace healing.

2. I am worthy of love and respect.

3. I forgive others and set myself free.

4. My past does not define my future.

5. I am strong, resilient, and capable.

6. I attract positivity and abundance into my life.

7. I let go of fear and walk in faith.

8. I am loved and cherished by a loving God.

9. I am a vessel of God's light and love.

10. I trust in the divine timing of my life.

11. I am at peace with my past.

12. I choose joy and happiness every day.

13.I am worthy of all the blessings coming my way.

14.I am in control of my thoughts and emotions.

15.I release negativity and embrace positivity.

16.I am grateful for the lessons I've learned.

17.I radiate love and kindness to others.

18.I am surrounded by a supportive community.

19.I am constantly growing and evolving.

20.I attract healthy and loving relationships.

21.I am confident and believe in myself.

22.I let go of all regrets and guilt.

23.I am a magnet for divine healing energy.

24.I am free from the chains of my past.

25.I am exactly where I need to be in life.

The scriptures contain divine wisdom and offer solace, serving as reminders of God's unwavering love and His promises to mend the brokenhearted.

Scriptures

1. Psalm 34:18 - "The Lord is close to the brokenhearted and saves those who are crushed in spirit."

2. Isaiah 41:10 - "Fear not, for I am with you; be not dismayed, for I am your God; I will strengthen you, I will help you, I will uphold you with my righteous right hand."

3. Psalm 147:3 - "He heals the brokenhearted and binds up their wounds."

4. Jeremiah 29:11 - "For I know the plans I have for you, declares the Lord, plans for welfare and not for evil, to give you a future and a hope."

5. 2 Corinthians 12:9 - "My grace is sufficient for you, for my power is made perfect in weakness."

6. Philippians 4:13 - "I can do all things through him who strengthens me."

7. Romans 8:28 - "And we know that in all things God works for the good of those who love him, who have been called according to his purpose."

8. Proverbs 3:5-6 - "Trust in the Lord with all your heart, and do not lean on your own understanding. In all your ways acknowledge him, and he will make straight your paths."

9. Matthew 11:28-30 - "Come to me, all who labor and are heavy laden, and I will give you rest. Take my yoke upon you, and learn from me, for I am gentle and lowly in heart, and you will find rest for your souls."

10.Psalm 30:2 - "Lord my God, I called to you for help, and you healed me."

11.Romans 15:13 - "May the God of hope fill you with all joy and peace in believing, so that by the power of the Holy Spirit you may abound in hope."

12.James 1:2-4 - "Count it all joy, my brothers, when you meet trials of various kinds, for you know that the testing of your faith produces steadfastness. And let steadfastness have its full effect, that you may be perfect and complete, lacking in nothing."

13.Psalm 51:10 - "Create in me a clean heart, O God, and renew a right spirit within me."

14. 1 Peter 5:7 - "Casting all your anxieties on him, because he cares for you."

15. Romans 12:2 - "Do not be conformed to this world, but be transformed by the renewal of your mind, that by testing you may discern what is the will of God, what is good and acceptable and perfect."

16. Isaiah 53:5 - "But he was pierced for our transgressions; he was crushed for our iniquities; upon him was the chastisement that brought us peace, and with his wounds, we are healed."

17. Psalm 119:105 - "Your word is a lamp to my feet and a light to my path."

18. Romans 8:37 - "No, in all these things, we are more than conquerors through him who loved us."

19. Ephesians 4:31-32 - "Let all bitterness and wrath and anger and clamor and slander be put away from you, along with all malice. Be kind to one another, tenderhearted, forgiving one another, as God in Christ forgave you."

20. 2 Timothy 1:7 - "For God gave us a spirit not of fear but

of power and love and self-control."

21.Psalm 55:22 - "Cast your burden on the Lord, and he will sustain you; he will never permit the righteous to be moved."

22.John 14:27 - "Peace I leave with you; my peace I give to you. Not as the world gives do I give to you. Let not your hearts be troubled, neither let them be afraid."

23.Psalm 37:4 - "Delight yourself in the Lord, and he will give you the desires of your heart."

24.Romans 5:1 - "Therefore, since we have been justified by faith, we have peace with God through our Lord Jesus Christ."

25.Psalm 139:14 - "I praise you because I am fearfully and wonderfully made; your works are wonderful, I know that full well."

I hope you find strength and inspiration in these affirmations and scriptures as you continue on your path towards healing and wholeness.

Chapter 7

All hearts and Cats Clear?

In the end, what truly matters is your progress and growth. The journey you've embarked on is deeply personal, and the path to healing and wholeness is unique for each of us. So, as you reflect on the wisdom shared within these pages, ask yourself: "Do I believe I can put my Cat on the altar? Was this journey helpful?" Your answers to these questions are the compass guiding you toward a future full of hope, faith, and love.

I wish you the very best on this continued journey of healing and self-discovery. As you move forward, remember to keep that Cat on the altar, just like Forrest Gump, run like your life depends on it, away from situations and circumstances that might hinder your progress.

With much love and faith in your ability to heal and grow, I say to you: Keep putting your Cat on the altar and let God guide your path. I invite you to share your thoughts on this book, your progress in KEEPING THAT CAT on the Altar. I really want to hear from you. Please feel free to email me at llove@lashawndashiree.info, and let's continue this journey together.

Thank you for allowing me to be a part of your journey.

With love and blessings,

Dr. Lashawnda Love

Lashawnda
SHIREE
I AM ME

MEET THE AUTHOR

Lashawnda Shiree Love is a multi-talented individual who wears many hats. She's a wife, a loving mother of three children - Chadrick Leshane Kyles (22), Shedrick Nayshon Kyles (18), and Purpose Lovel Lamb (9). She's also an accomplished entrepreneur, a dedicated business owner, a minister, a community service provider, an author, a ghostwriter, a YouTube Vlogger, a makeup artist, a gospel recording artist, and the CEO and founder of Mama Tees Catering LLC, where she serves as the Personal Chef, specializing in crafting exquisite keto meal preps and a delectable array of home-cooked meals.

Lashawnda is the CEO of Intellectual Designs by Lashawnda Love, a Social Media Marketing company. She's the founder of her own publishing company, Stork Publishing

LLC. Dr. Love can be attributed to helping numerous individuals bring their creative visions to life in the form of books or journals, either as a writer or ghostwriter.

In her career, she's created magazines for renowned publications such as Mogul Leaders Magazine, N.B.Q Magazine, and crafted various graphics for K.I.S.H. Magazine. Lashawnda specializes in creating websites, developing social media content, and offering social media training. She's a digital creator and the brains behind her cosmetics line, "Lashawnda Shiree."

Lashawnda is not just an entrepreneur; she's also a Life Coach and Mentor, offering guidance through her platform "Let's Talk About It." With a Doctorate in Christian Counseling, she works as a Therapist at Clearpath and Professional Associates HealthCare of Georgia. She is the visionary behind B.A.B.Y. Ministry (Becoming A Better You) where she passionately seeks to save souls, heal marriages, and break chains.

Having been through two failed marriages, Lashawnda understands the importance of healing and breaking destructive cycles. She overcame abuse and violence and emerged stronger. Through divine intervention, her husband

David Hassan Habbi Love found her on January 7, 2022, and they became husband and wife on March 29, 2022. Lashawnda's mission is to promote the kingdom of God through preaching, teaching, praise, and worship, supporting women who have been through hardship, and inspiring others to let their light shine.

Lashawnda is also a talented singer and songwriter with several singles to her name, including "Deeper," "The Perfect Gift," "Because of Who You Are," and "Silent Night." Her newest compilation, "Kingdom Ambassadors Ministries Family & Dr. Delesa Patterson Prophetic Release Prayer for Our Nation," reflects her dedication to spiritual endeavors. She is also the author of the book "Put Your Cat on the Altar: A Guide to Winning the War Against a Narcissist" and the book "Rock Your Spouse World 7 Days out of the Month," which she co-authored with Dr. Erica Thomas. Her agenda "Just a Girl Who Survived and Decided to Build Her Empire" exemplifies her resilience.

In collaboration with her husband, Lashawnda has created journals and a T-shirt line known as "The Loves Collection," which includes journals for couples, "Black Love Matters," and "I am Black History."

Lashawnda has been a featured guest speaker on numerous social media platforms, sharing her insights on various topics related to marriage, affairs, divorce, and remarriage. She has been prominently featured in KISH Magazine, Mogul Leaders Magazine, and even graced the front cover of NBQ Magazine.

You can connect with Lashawnda on various social media platforms:

- Facebook: Lashawnda Love

- Facebook Business Page: Intellectual Designs by Lashawnda Shiree

- Instagram: LashawndaShireeLove YouTube: Lashawnda Shiree LoveTik Tok: Dr Lashawndalove

- Email: llove@lashawndashiree.info

- Phone Number: 334-232-9281

- Websites: www.lashawndashiree.info, www.payhip/lashawndashiree, www.lovescollection.com, bit.ly/3UGzLOo

Love

THE LOVES

EST 2022

B.A.B.Y.
BABY

Love
THE LOVES
EST 2022

inte**L**ectual Designs

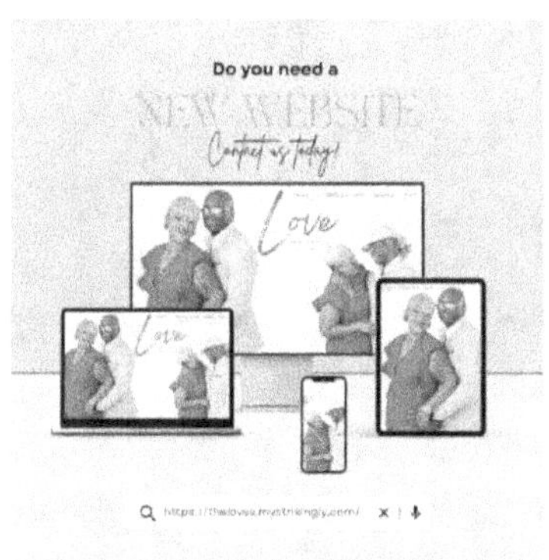

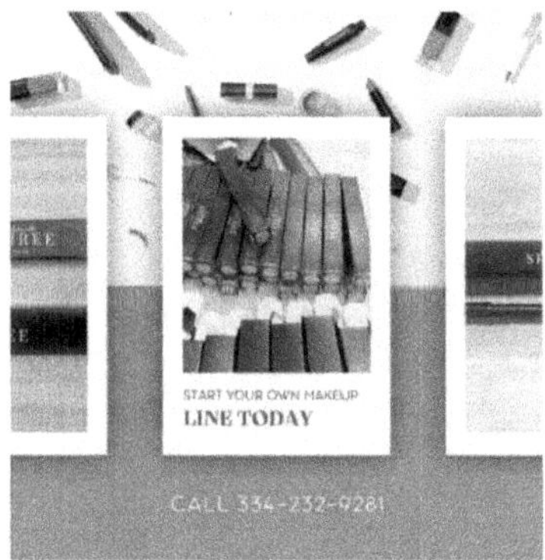

If you are interested in any of these services please visit
(www.lashawndashiree.info/intellectualdesigns) for more information.

If you would like to purchase Lipstick and Lip Liners please
visit (www.payhip.com/lashawndashiree)

Love
COLLECTION
BLACK
LOVE
MATTERS
www.lovescollection.com

Thank You

Dear Reader,

As you reach the end of this book, I want to express my profound gratitude for joining me on this transformative journey. Your commitment to exploring these pages and embracing the messages within reflects your dedication to self-discovery, healing, and spiritual growth.

Thank you for making this voyage with me. I trust you found inspiration, encouragement, and strength throughout this book. Remember, the power of healing, renewal, and living life to its fullest is within your grasp.

Your thoughts, experiences, and progress in Keeping That Cat on the Altar are valuable. Please connect with me and share your journey at llove@lashawndashiree.info. Your stories and insights can be a source of inspiration and encouragement to others as they travel their own paths to wholeness.

With sincere appreciation,

Dr. Lashawnda Love